50 Homemade Pizza Perfection Recipes for Home

By: Kelly Johnson

Table of Contents

- Margherita Pizza
- Pepperoni and Mushroom Pizza
- BBQ Chicken Pizza
- Mediterranean Veggie Pizza
- Hawaiian Pizza
- Buffalo Chicken Pizza
- Pesto and Cherry Tomato Pizza
- Spinach and Feta Pizza
- White Pizza with Ricotta and Garlic
- Prosciutto and Arugula Pizza
- Caprese Pizza
- Sausage and Peppers Pizza
- Fig and Gorgonzola Pizza
- Shrimp Scampi Pizza
- Taco Pizza
- Philly Cheesesteak Pizza
- Breakfast Pizza with Eggs and Bacon
- Artichoke and Olive Pizza
- Roasted Red Pepper and Goat Cheese Pizza
- Truffle Mushroom Pizza
- Chicken Alfredo Pizza
- Meat Lover's Pizza
- Caramelized Onion and Brie Pizza
- BLT Pizza
- Shrimp and Pesto Pizza
- Margherita with Balsamic Glaze
- Mediterranean Hummus Pizza
- Buffalo Cauliflower Pizza
- Greek Gyro Pizza
- BBQ Pulled Pork Pizza
- Thai Chicken Pizza
- Caramelized Pear and Gorgonzola Pizza
- Smoked Salmon and Cream Cheese Pizza
- Ratatouille Pizza
- Chipotle BBQ Beef Pizza

- Bruschetta Pizza
- Apple, Bacon, and Cheddar Pizza
- S'mores Dessert Pizza
- Roasted Veggie and Pesto Pizza
- Buffalo Cauliflower Ranch Pizza
- Chicken Tikka Masala Pizza
- Pear and Prosciutto Pizza
- Spinach and Artichoke Dip Pizza
- Caramelized Apple and Brie Dessert Pizza
- Caprese with Pesto Drizzle
- Mediterranean Chicken Flatbread
- Roasted Garlic and Potato Pizza
- Fig, Prosciutto, and Gorgonzola Flatbread
- Zucchini and Goat Cheese Pizza
- Pumpkin and Sage Pizza

Margherita Pizza

Ingredients:

For the Pizza Dough:

- 2 1/4 teaspoons (1 packet) active dry yeast
- 1 teaspoon sugar
- 1 cup warm water (about 110°F or 43°C)
- 2 1/2 cups all-purpose flour
- 1 teaspoon salt
- 1 tablespoon olive oil

For the Pizza Toppings:

- 1 cup tomato sauce (homemade or store-bought)
- 8 ounces fresh mozzarella cheese, sliced
- Fresh basil leaves
- Extra-virgin olive oil, for drizzling
- Salt and pepper, to taste

Instructions:

1. Prepare the Pizza Dough:

    In a small bowl, combine the active dry yeast, sugar, and warm water. Let it sit for about 5 minutes, or until it becomes frothy.
    In a large mixing bowl, combine the flour and salt. Make a well in the center and add the yeast mixture and olive oil. Mix until a dough forms.
    Knead the dough on a floured surface for about 5-7 minutes until it becomes smooth and elastic.
    Place the dough in a lightly oiled bowl, cover it with a kitchen towel, and let it rise in a warm place for 1-2 hours or until it doubles in size.

2. Preheat the Oven:

    Preheat your oven to the highest temperature it can reach (usually around 500°F or 260°C). If you have a pizza stone, place it in the oven while preheating.

3. Roll Out the Dough:

    Punch down the risen dough and divide it into two portions. Roll out each portion on a floured surface to your desired thickness.

4. Assemble the Pizza:

   If using a pizza stone, transfer the rolled-out dough onto a piece of parchment paper.
   Spread a thin layer of tomato sauce over the dough, leaving a small border around the edges.
   Arrange slices of fresh mozzarella evenly on top of the sauce.
   Tear fresh basil leaves and scatter them over the pizza.
   Drizzle with extra-virgin olive oil and sprinkle with salt and pepper.

5. Bake the Pizza:

   If using a pizza stone, carefully transfer the parchment paper with the assembled pizza onto the preheated stone. If not using a stone, place the pizza directly on a baking sheet.
   Bake in the preheated oven for about 10-12 minutes or until the crust is golden and the cheese is melted and bubbly.
   Remove the pizza from the oven and let it cool for a few minutes before slicing.
   Repeat the process for the second portion of dough.

6. Serve:

   Slice the Margherita pizza and serve it hot. Optionally, garnish with additional fresh basil leaves.

Enjoy your homemade Margherita pizza, showcasing the classic combination of tomato, mozzarella, and basil!

Pepperoni and Mushroom Pizza

Ingredients:

For the Pizza Dough:

- 2 1/4 teaspoons (1 packet) active dry yeast
- 1 teaspoon sugar
- 1 cup warm water (about 110°F or 43°C)
- 2 1/2 cups all-purpose flour
- 1 teaspoon salt
- 1 tablespoon olive oil

For the Pizza Toppings:

- 1 cup tomato sauce (homemade or store-bought)
- 1 1/2 cups shredded mozzarella cheese
- Pepperoni slices
- 1 cup sliced mushrooms
- 1/2 teaspoon dried oregano
- Crushed red pepper flakes (optional)
- Olive oil, for drizzling

Instructions:

1. Prepare the Pizza Dough:

   In a small bowl, combine the active dry yeast, sugar, and warm water. Allow it to sit for about 5 minutes, or until it becomes frothy.
   In a large mixing bowl, combine the flour and salt. Make a well in the center and add the yeast mixture and olive oil. Mix until a dough forms.
   Knead the dough on a floured surface for about 5-7 minutes until it becomes smooth and elastic.
   Place the dough in a lightly oiled bowl, cover it with a kitchen towel, and let it rise in a warm place for 1-2 hours or until it doubles in size.

2. Preheat the Oven:

   Preheat your oven to the highest temperature it can reach (usually around 500°F or 260°C). If you have a pizza stone, place it in the oven while preheating.

3. Roll Out the Dough:

   Punch down the risen dough and roll it out on a floured surface to your desired thickness.

4. Assemble the Pizza:

   If using a pizza stone, transfer the rolled-out dough onto a piece of parchment paper.
   Spread a layer of tomato sauce over the dough, leaving a small border around the edges.
   Sprinkle shredded mozzarella evenly over the sauce.
   Arrange pepperoni slices and sliced mushrooms over the cheese.
   Sprinkle dried oregano and, if desired, crushed red pepper flakes over the toppings.

5. Bake the Pizza:

   If using a pizza stone, carefully transfer the parchment paper with the assembled pizza onto the preheated stone. If not using a stone, place the pizza directly on a baking sheet.
   Bake in the preheated oven for about 10-12 minutes or until the crust is golden and the cheese is melted and bubbly.

6. Serve:

   Drizzle olive oil over the hot pizza, slice, and serve immediately.

Enjoy your homemade Pepperoni and Mushroom Pizza with the perfect balance of flavors!

BBQ Chicken Pizza

Ingredients:

For the Pizza Dough:

- 2 1/4 teaspoons (1 packet) active dry yeast
- 1 teaspoon sugar
- 1 cup warm water (about 110°F or 43°C)
- 2 1/2 cups all-purpose flour
- 1 teaspoon salt
- 1 tablespoon olive oil

For the Pizza Toppings:

- 1/2 cup barbecue sauce (homemade or store-bought)
- 1 1/2 cups cooked and shredded chicken breast
- 1 1/2 cups shredded mozzarella cheese
- 1/4 red onion, thinly sliced
- 1/4 cup chopped fresh cilantro
- Olive oil, for drizzling

Instructions:

1. Prepare the Pizza Dough:

    In a small bowl, combine the active dry yeast, sugar, and warm water. Allow it to sit for about 5 minutes, or until it becomes frothy.
    In a large mixing bowl, combine the flour and salt. Make a well in the center and add the yeast mixture and olive oil. Mix until a dough forms.
    Knead the dough on a floured surface for about 5-7 minutes until it becomes smooth and elastic.
    Place the dough in a lightly oiled bowl, cover it with a kitchen towel, and let it rise in a warm place for 1-2 hours or until it doubles in size.

2. Preheat the Oven:

    Preheat your oven to the highest temperature it can reach (usually around 500°F or 260°C). If you have a pizza stone, place it in the oven while preheating.

3. Roll Out the Dough:

Punch down the risen dough and roll it out on a floured surface to your desired thickness.

4. Assemble the Pizza:

    If using a pizza stone, transfer the rolled-out dough onto a piece of parchment paper.
    Spread a layer of barbecue sauce over the dough, leaving a small border around the edges.
    Sprinkle shredded mozzarella evenly over the sauce.
    Scatter shredded chicken evenly over the cheese.
    Add sliced red onions on top.

5. Bake the Pizza:

    If using a pizza stone, carefully transfer the parchment paper with the assembled pizza onto the preheated stone. If not using a stone, place the pizza directly on a baking sheet.
    Bake in the preheated oven for about 10-12 minutes or until the crust is golden, the cheese is melted, and the edges are slightly crispy.

6. Garnish and Serve:

    Once out of the oven, drizzle olive oil over the hot pizza.
    Sprinkle chopped cilantro on top for freshness.
    Slice and serve your delicious BBQ Chicken Pizza.

Enjoy your homemade BBQ Chicken Pizza with the smoky and savory flavors of barbecue sauce!

Mediterranean Veggie Pizza

Ingredients:

For the Pizza Dough:

- 2 1/4 teaspoons (1 packet) active dry yeast
- 1 teaspoon sugar
- 1 cup warm water (about 110°F or 43°C)
- 2 1/2 cups all-purpose flour
- 1 teaspoon salt
- 1 tablespoon olive oil

For the Pizza Toppings:

- 1/2 cup hummus (store-bought or homemade)
- 1 1/2 cups cherry tomatoes, halved
- 1 cup sliced black olives
- 1 cup crumbled feta cheese
- 1/2 cup red onion, thinly sliced
- 1/4 cup chopped fresh basil
- Olive oil, for drizzling

Instructions:

1. Prepare the Pizza Dough:

    In a small bowl, combine the active dry yeast, sugar, and warm water. Allow it to sit for about 5 minutes, or until it becomes frothy.
    In a large mixing bowl, combine the flour and salt. Make a well in the center and add the yeast mixture and olive oil. Mix until a dough forms.
    Knead the dough on a floured surface for about 5-7 minutes until it becomes smooth and elastic.
    Place the dough in a lightly oiled bowl, cover it with a kitchen towel, and let it rise in a warm place for 1-2 hours or until it doubles in size.

2. Preheat the Oven:

    Preheat your oven to the highest temperature it can reach (usually around 500°F or 260°C). If you have a pizza stone, place it in the oven while preheating.

3. Roll Out the Dough:

Punch down the risen dough and roll it out on a floured surface to your desired thickness.

4. Assemble the Pizza:

If using a pizza stone, transfer the rolled-out dough onto a piece of parchment paper. Spread a layer of hummus over the dough, leaving a small border around the edges. Scatter halved cherry tomatoes, sliced black olives, crumbled feta cheese, and thinly sliced red onion over the hummus.

5. Bake the Pizza:

If using a pizza stone, carefully transfer the parchment paper with the assembled pizza onto the preheated stone. If not using a stone, place the pizza directly on a baking sheet. Bake in the preheated oven for about 10-12 minutes or until the crust is golden and the toppings are heated through.

6. Garnish and Serve:

Once out of the oven, drizzle olive oil over the hot pizza.
Sprinkle chopped fresh basil on top for added freshness.
Slice and serve your delightful Mediterranean Veggie Pizza.

Enjoy your homemade Mediterranean Veggie Pizza, featuring the vibrant and healthy flavors of the Mediterranean region!

Hawaiian Pizza

Ingredients:

For the Pizza Dough:

- 2 1/4 teaspoons (1 packet) active dry yeast
- 1 teaspoon sugar
- 1 cup warm water (about 110°F or 43°C)
- 2 1/2 cups all-purpose flour
- 1 teaspoon salt
- 1 tablespoon olive oil

For the Pizza Toppings:

- 1/2 cup pizza sauce (homemade or store-bought)
- 1 1/2 cups shredded mozzarella cheese
- 1 cup diced cooked ham
- 1 cup pineapple chunks, drained
- 1/4 cup red onion, thinly sliced (optional)
- 1/4 cup chopped fresh cilantro or parsley (optional)
- Olive oil, for drizzling

Instructions:

1. Prepare the Pizza Dough:

    In a small bowl, combine the active dry yeast, sugar, and warm water. Allow it to sit for about 5 minutes, or until it becomes frothy.
    In a large mixing bowl, combine the flour and salt. Make a well in the center and add the yeast mixture and olive oil. Mix until a dough forms.
    Knead the dough on a floured surface for about 5-7 minutes until it becomes smooth and elastic.
    Place the dough in a lightly oiled bowl, cover it with a kitchen towel, and let it rise in a warm place for 1-2 hours or until it doubles in size.

2. Preheat the Oven:

    Preheat your oven to the highest temperature it can reach (usually around 500°F or 260°C). If you have a pizza stone, place it in the oven while preheating.

3. Roll Out the Dough:

Punch down the risen dough and roll it out on a floured surface to your desired thickness.

4. Assemble the Pizza:

   If using a pizza stone, transfer the rolled-out dough onto a piece of parchment paper.
   Spread a layer of pizza sauce over the dough, leaving a small border around the edges.
   Sprinkle shredded mozzarella evenly over the sauce.
   Scatter diced ham, pineapple chunks, and optionally sliced red onion over the cheese.

5. Bake the Pizza:

   If using a pizza stone, carefully transfer the parchment paper with the assembled pizza onto the preheated stone. If not using a stone, place the pizza directly on a baking sheet.
   Bake in the preheated oven for about 10-12 minutes or until the crust is golden and the cheese is melted and bubbly.

6. Garnish and Serve:

   Once out of the oven, drizzle olive oil over the hot pizza.
   Optionally, sprinkle chopped fresh cilantro or parsley on top.
   Slice and serve your delicious Hawaiian Pizza.

Enjoy your homemade Hawaiian Pizza, featuring the perfect balance of sweetness from pineapple and savory goodness from ham!

Buffalo Chicken Pizza

Ingredients:

For the Pizza Dough:

- 2 1/4 teaspoons (1 packet) active dry yeast
- 1 teaspoon sugar
- 1 cup warm water (about 110°F or 43°C)
- 2 1/2 cups all-purpose flour
- 1 teaspoon salt
- 1 tablespoon olive oil

For the Pizza Toppings:

- 1/2 cup buffalo sauce (store-bought or homemade)
- 1 1/2 cups cooked and shredded chicken breast
- 1 1/2 cups shredded mozzarella cheese
- 1/4 cup blue cheese crumbles
- 1/4 cup ranch or blue cheese dressing
- 2 tablespoons chopped green onions (optional)
- Olive oil, for drizzling

Instructions:

1. Prepare the Pizza Dough:

   In a small bowl, combine the active dry yeast, sugar, and warm water. Allow it to sit for about 5 minutes, or until it becomes frothy.
   In a large mixing bowl, combine the flour and salt. Make a well in the center and add the yeast mixture and olive oil. Mix until a dough forms.
   Knead the dough on a floured surface for about 5-7 minutes until it becomes smooth and elastic.
   Place the dough in a lightly oiled bowl, cover it with a kitchen towel, and let it rise in a warm place for 1-2 hours or until it doubles in size.

2. Preheat the Oven:

   Preheat your oven to the highest temperature it can reach (usually around 500°F or 260°C). If you have a pizza stone, place it in the oven while preheating.

3. Roll Out the Dough:

Punch down the risen dough and roll it out on a floured surface to your desired thickness.

4. Assemble the Pizza:

>If using a pizza stone, transfer the rolled-out dough onto a piece of parchment paper.
>Spread a layer of buffalo sauce over the dough, leaving a small border around the edges.
>Sprinkle shredded mozzarella evenly over the sauce.
>Scatter shredded chicken evenly over the cheese.
>Add blue cheese crumbles on top.

5. Bake the Pizza:

>If using a pizza stone, carefully transfer the parchment paper with the assembled pizza onto the preheated stone. If not using a stone, place the pizza directly on a baking sheet.
>Bake in the preheated oven for about 10-12 minutes or until the crust is golden, the cheese is melted, and the edges are slightly crispy.

6. Garnish and Serve:

>Once out of the oven, drizzle olive oil over the hot pizza.
>Drizzle ranch or blue cheese dressing over the top.
>Optionally, sprinkle chopped green onions for added freshness.
>Slice and serve your delicious Buffalo Chicken Pizza.

Enjoy your homemade Buffalo Chicken Pizza with the perfect blend of spicy buffalo sauce and cool blue cheese dressing!

Pesto and Cherry Tomato Pizza

Ingredients:

For the Pizza Dough:

- 2 1/4 teaspoons (1 packet) active dry yeast
- 1 teaspoon sugar
- 1 cup warm water (about 110°F or 43°C)
- 2 1/2 cups all-purpose flour
- 1 teaspoon salt
- 1 tablespoon olive oil

For the Pizza Toppings:

- 1/2 cup basil pesto (store-bought or homemade)
- 1 1/2 cups cherry tomatoes, halved
- 1 1/2 cups shredded mozzarella cheese
- 1/4 cup grated Parmesan cheese
- Fresh basil leaves, for garnish
- Olive oil, for drizzling

Instructions:

1. Prepare the Pizza Dough:

    In a small bowl, combine the active dry yeast, sugar, and warm water. Allow it to sit for about 5 minutes, or until it becomes frothy.
    In a large mixing bowl, combine the flour and salt. Make a well in the center and add the yeast mixture and olive oil. Mix until a dough forms.
    Knead the dough on a floured surface for about 5-7 minutes until it becomes smooth and elastic.
    Place the dough in a lightly oiled bowl, cover it with a kitchen towel, and let it rise in a warm place for 1-2 hours or until it doubles in size.

2. Preheat the Oven:

    Preheat your oven to the highest temperature it can reach (usually around 500°F or 260°C). If you have a pizza stone, place it in the oven while preheating.

3. Roll Out the Dough:

Punch down the risen dough and roll it out on a floured surface to your desired thickness.

4. Assemble the Pizza:

   If using a pizza stone, transfer the rolled-out dough onto a piece of parchment paper.
   Spread a layer of basil pesto over the dough, leaving a small border around the edges.
   Sprinkle shredded mozzarella evenly over the pesto.
   Arrange halved cherry tomatoes on top of the cheese.
   Sprinkle grated Parmesan cheese over the tomatoes.

5. Bake the Pizza:

   If using a pizza stone, carefully transfer the parchment paper with the assembled pizza onto the preheated stone. If not using a stone, place the pizza directly on a baking sheet.
   Bake in the preheated oven for about 10-12 minutes or until the crust is golden, the cheese is melted, and the edges are slightly crispy.

6. Garnish and Serve:

   Once out of the oven, drizzle olive oil over the hot pizza.
   Garnish with fresh basil leaves for added freshness.
   Slice and serve your delicious Pesto and Cherry Tomato Pizza.

Enjoy your homemade pizza with the wonderful combination of pesto, cherry tomatoes, and melted cheese!

Spinach and Feta Pizza

Ingredients:

For the Pizza Dough:

- 2 1/4 teaspoons (1 packet) active dry yeast
- 1 teaspoon sugar
- 1 cup warm water (about 110°F or 43°C)
- 2 1/2 cups all-purpose flour
- 1 teaspoon salt
- 1 tablespoon olive oil

For the Pizza Toppings:

- 1/2 cup pizza sauce (homemade or store-bought)
- 2 cups fresh baby spinach leaves
- 1 cup crumbled feta cheese
- 1/2 cup shredded mozzarella cheese
- 1/4 cup grated Parmesan cheese
- 1 clove garlic, minced
- Red pepper flakes (optional)
- Olive oil, for drizzling

Instructions:

1. Prepare the Pizza Dough:

    In a small bowl, combine the active dry yeast, sugar, and warm water. Allow it to sit for about 5 minutes, or until it becomes frothy.
    In a large mixing bowl, combine the flour and salt. Make a well in the center and add the yeast mixture and olive oil. Mix until a dough forms.
    Knead the dough on a floured surface for about 5-7 minutes until it becomes smooth and elastic.
    Place the dough in a lightly oiled bowl, cover it with a kitchen towel, and let it rise in a warm place for 1-2 hours or until it doubles in size.

2. Preheat the Oven:

    Preheat your oven to the highest temperature it can reach (usually around 500°F or 260°C). If you have a pizza stone, place it in the oven while preheating.

3. Roll Out the Dough:

   Punch down the risen dough and roll it out on a floured surface to your desired thickness.

4. Assemble the Pizza:

   If using a pizza stone, transfer the rolled-out dough onto a piece of parchment paper.
   Spread a layer of pizza sauce over the dough, leaving a small border around the edges.
   Scatter fresh baby spinach leaves evenly over the sauce.
   Sprinkle crumbled feta cheese, shredded mozzarella cheese, and grated Parmesan cheese over the spinach.
   Distribute minced garlic evenly over the toppings.

5. Bake the Pizza:

   If using a pizza stone, carefully transfer the parchment paper with the assembled pizza onto the preheated stone. If not using a stone, place the pizza directly on a baking sheet.
   Bake in the preheated oven for about 10-12 minutes or until the crust is golden, the cheese is melted, and the edges are slightly crispy.

6. Garnish and Serve:

   Once out of the oven, drizzle olive oil over the hot pizza.
   Optionally, sprinkle red pepper flakes for a touch of heat.
   Slice and serve your delicious Spinach and Feta Pizza.

Enjoy your homemade pizza with the delightful combination of spinach, feta, and melted cheese!

White Pizza with Ricotta and Garlic

Ingredients:

For the Pizza Dough:

- 2 1/4 teaspoons (1 packet) active dry yeast
- 1 teaspoon sugar
- 1 cup warm water (about 110°F or 43°C)
- 2 1/2 cups all-purpose flour
- 1 teaspoon salt
- 1 tablespoon olive oil

For the White Pizza Toppings:

- 1 cup whole milk ricotta cheese
- 1 cup shredded mozzarella cheese
- 1/2 cup grated Parmesan cheese
- 3 cloves garlic, minced
- Fresh basil leaves, for garnish
- Olive oil, for drizzling

Instructions:

1. Prepare the Pizza Dough:

    In a small bowl, combine the active dry yeast, sugar, and warm water. Allow it to sit for about 5 minutes, or until it becomes frothy.
    In a large mixing bowl, combine the flour and salt. Make a well in the center and add the yeast mixture and olive oil. Mix until a dough forms.
    Knead the dough on a floured surface for about 5-7 minutes until it becomes smooth and elastic.
    Place the dough in a lightly oiled bowl, cover it with a kitchen towel, and let it rise in a warm place for 1-2 hours or until it doubles in size.

2. Preheat the Oven:

    Preheat your oven to the highest temperature it can reach (usually around 500°F or 260°C). If you have a pizza stone, place it in the oven while preheating.

3. Roll Out the Dough:

Punch down the risen dough and roll it out on a floured surface to your desired thickness.

4. Assemble the White Pizza:

   If using a pizza stone, transfer the rolled-out dough onto a piece of parchment paper.
   Spread an even layer of ricotta cheese over the dough, leaving a small border around the edges.
   Sprinkle shredded mozzarella and grated Parmesan evenly over the ricotta.
   Distribute minced garlic evenly over the toppings.

5. Bake the White Pizza:

   If using a pizza stone, carefully transfer the parchment paper with the assembled pizza onto the preheated stone. If not using a stone, place the pizza directly on a baking sheet.
   Bake in the preheated oven for about 10-12 minutes or until the crust is golden, the cheese is melted, and the edges are slightly crispy.

6. Garnish and Serve:

   Once out of the oven, drizzle olive oil over the hot pizza.
   Garnish with fresh basil leaves for added freshness.
   Slice and serve your delicious White Pizza with Ricotta and Garlic.

Enjoy your homemade pizza with the creamy richness of ricotta and the aromatic flavor of garlic!

Prosciutto and Arugula Pizza

Ingredients:

For the Pizza Dough:

- 2 1/4 teaspoons (1 packet) active dry yeast
- 1 teaspoon sugar
- 1 cup warm water (about 110°F or 43°C)
- 2 1/2 cups all-purpose flour
- 1 teaspoon salt
- 1 tablespoon olive oil

For the Pizza Toppings:

- 1/2 cup pizza sauce (homemade or store-bought)
- 1 1/2 cups shredded mozzarella cheese
- 4-6 slices of prosciutto
- 2 cups fresh arugula
- 1 tablespoon balsamic glaze (optional)
- Olive oil, for drizzling

Instructions:

1. Prepare the Pizza Dough:

    In a small bowl, combine the active dry yeast, sugar, and warm water. Allow it to sit for about 5 minutes, or until it becomes frothy.
    In a large mixing bowl, combine the flour and salt. Make a well in the center and add the yeast mixture and olive oil. Mix until a dough forms.
    Knead the dough on a floured surface for about 5-7 minutes until it becomes smooth and elastic.
    Place the dough in a lightly oiled bowl, cover it with a kitchen towel, and let it rise in a warm place for 1-2 hours or until it doubles in size.

2. Preheat the Oven:

    Preheat your oven to the highest temperature it can reach (usually around 500°F or 260°C). If you have a pizza stone, place it in the oven while preheating.

3. Roll Out the Dough:

Punch down the risen dough and roll it out on a floured surface to your desired thickness.

4. Assemble the Pizza:

If using a pizza stone, transfer the rolled-out dough onto a piece of parchment paper.
Spread a layer of pizza sauce over the dough, leaving a small border around the edges.
Sprinkle shredded mozzarella evenly over the sauce.
Arrange slices of prosciutto on top of the cheese.

5. Bake the Pizza:

If using a pizza stone, carefully transfer the parchment paper with the assembled pizza onto the preheated stone. If not using a stone, place the pizza directly on a baking sheet.
Bake in the preheated oven for about 10-12 minutes or until the crust is golden, the cheese is melted, and the edges are slightly crispy.

6. Finish and Serve:

Once out of the oven, top the pizza with fresh arugula.
Drizzle olive oil over the arugula and the entire pizza.
Optionally, drizzle balsamic glaze over the top for added flavor.
Slice and serve your delicious Prosciutto and Arugula Pizza.

Enjoy the wonderful combination of salty prosciutto, peppery arugula, and melted cheese on this gourmet pizza!

Caprese Pizza

Ingredients:

For the Pizza Dough:

- 2 1/4 teaspoons (1 packet) active dry yeast
- 1 teaspoon sugar
- 1 cup warm water (about 110°F or 43°C)
- 2 1/2 cups all-purpose flour
- 1 teaspoon salt
- 1 tablespoon olive oil

For the Caprese Pizza Toppings:

- 1/2 cup pizza sauce (homemade or store-bought)
- 1 1/2 cups fresh mozzarella, sliced
- 2-3 large tomatoes, thinly sliced
- Fresh basil leaves
- Balsamic glaze, for drizzling
- Salt and pepper, to taste
- Olive oil, for drizzling

Instructions:

1. Prepare the Pizza Dough:

    In a small bowl, combine the active dry yeast, sugar, and warm water. Allow it to sit for about 5 minutes, or until it becomes frothy.
    In a large mixing bowl, combine the flour and salt. Make a well in the center and add the yeast mixture and olive oil. Mix until a dough forms.
    Knead the dough on a floured surface for about 5-7 minutes until it becomes smooth and elastic.
    Place the dough in a lightly oiled bowl, cover it with a kitchen towel, and let it rise in a warm place for 1-2 hours or until it doubles in size.

2. Preheat the Oven:

    Preheat your oven to the highest temperature it can reach (usually around 500°F or 260°C). If you have a pizza stone, place it in the oven while preheating.

3. Roll Out the Dough:

Punch down the risen dough and roll it out on a floured surface to your desired thickness.

4. Assemble the Caprese Pizza:

If using a pizza stone, transfer the rolled-out dough onto a piece of parchment paper.
Spread a layer of pizza sauce over the dough, leaving a small border around the edges.
Arrange slices of fresh mozzarella and tomatoes evenly over the sauce.
Sprinkle salt and pepper to taste.

5. Bake the Pizza:

If using a pizza stone, carefully transfer the parchment paper with the assembled pizza onto the preheated stone. If not using a stone, place the pizza directly on a baking sheet.
Bake in the preheated oven for about 10-12 minutes or until the crust is golden, the cheese is melted, and the edges are slightly crispy.

6. Finish and Serve:

Once out of the oven, top the pizza with fresh basil leaves.
Drizzle olive oil and balsamic glaze over the top.
Slice and serve your delicious Caprese Pizza.

Enjoy the fresh and vibrant flavors of this classic Caprese Pizza!

Sausage and Peppers Pizza

Ingredients:

- Pizza dough (store-bought or homemade)
- Olive oil
- 1 cup tomato sauce
- 2 cups shredded mozzarella cheese
- 1/2 pound Italian sausage, cooked and crumbled
- 1 bell pepper, thinly sliced
- 1 onion, thinly sliced
- Salt and pepper to taste
- Red pepper flakes (optional, for added spice)
- Grated Parmesan cheese (optional, for topping)

Instructions:

1. Preheat your oven according to the pizza dough package instructions or your homemade dough recipe.
2. Roll out the pizza dough on a floured surface to your desired thickness.
3. Place the rolled-out dough on a pizza stone or a baking sheet.
4. Brush the dough with olive oil to prevent it from getting soggy.
5. Spread an even layer of tomato sauce over the dough, leaving a small border around the edges.
6. Sprinkle the shredded mozzarella cheese evenly over the sauce.
7. Distribute the cooked and crumbled Italian sausage over the cheese.
8. Arrange the sliced bell peppers and onions on top of the sausage.
9. Season the pizza with salt, pepper, and red pepper flakes if you like it spicy.
10. Bake the pizza in the preheated oven according to the dough instructions or until the crust is golden and the cheese is melted and bubbly.
11. Optional: Once out of the oven, sprinkle the pizza with grated Parmesan cheese for extra flavor.
12. Allow the pizza to cool for a few minutes before slicing and serving.

Enjoy your delicious sausage and peppers pizza! You can customize the recipe by adding other toppings or using your favorite pizza sauce for a unique twist.

Fig and Gorgonzola Pizza

Ingredients:

- Pizza dough (store-bought or homemade)
- Olive oil
- 1 cup fig preserves or fig jam
- 1 ½ cups crumbled Gorgonzola cheese
- ½ cup chopped walnuts
- Fresh arugula (optional, for topping)
- Balsamic glaze (optional, for drizzling)
- Salt and pepper to taste

Instructions:

- Preheat your oven according to the pizza dough package instructions or your homemade dough recipe.
- Roll out the pizza dough on a floured surface to your desired thickness.
- Place the rolled-out dough on a pizza stone or a baking sheet.
- Brush the dough with olive oil to prevent it from getting soggy.
- Spread an even layer of fig preserves or jam over the dough, leaving a small border around the edges.
- Sprinkle the crumbled Gorgonzola cheese evenly over the fig layer.
- Distribute the chopped walnuts over the cheese.
- Season the pizza with a pinch of salt and pepper.
- Bake the pizza in the preheated oven according to the dough instructions or until the crust is golden and the cheese is melted.
- Optional: Once out of the oven, top the pizza with fresh arugula for a peppery kick.
- Optional: Drizzle balsamic glaze over the pizza for a sweet and tangy finish.
- Allow the pizza to cool for a few minutes before slicing and serving.

This Fig and Gorgonzola pizza is a unique and delicious option that combines the sweetness of figs with the bold and creamy flavors of Gorgonzola. Enjoy experimenting with the toppings to suit your taste preferences!

Shrimp Scampi Pizza

Ingredients:

- Pizza dough (store-bought or homemade)
- Olive oil
- 2 tablespoons unsalted butter
- 4 cloves garlic, minced
- 1 pound large shrimp, peeled and deveined
- Salt and black pepper to taste
- Crushed red pepper flakes (optional, for added spice)
- 1/4 cup dry white wine
- 1 tablespoon freshly squeezed lemon juice
- 1 cup shredded mozzarella cheese
- 1/4 cup grated Parmesan cheese
- Fresh parsley, chopped (for garnish)

Instructions:

- Preheat your oven according to the pizza dough package instructions or your homemade dough recipe.
- Roll out the pizza dough on a floured surface to your desired thickness.
- Place the rolled-out dough on a pizza stone or a baking sheet.
- In a large skillet, melt the butter and add minced garlic over medium heat. Cook for about 1-2 minutes until the garlic becomes fragrant but not browned.
- Add the shrimp to the skillet, season with salt, black pepper, and red pepper flakes (if using). Cook for 2-3 minutes or until the shrimp turn pink.
- Pour in the white wine and lemon juice, stirring to combine. Cook for an additional 2 minutes or until the shrimp are fully cooked and the sauce has thickened slightly. Remove from heat.
- Brush olive oil over the pizza dough to prevent sogginess.
- Spread the shrimp and garlic mixture evenly over the pizza dough.
- Sprinkle the shredded mozzarella and grated Parmesan cheese over the shrimp.
- Bake the pizza in the preheated oven according to the dough instructions or until the crust is golden and the cheese is melted and bubbly.
- Once out of the oven, garnish with freshly chopped parsley.
- Allow the pizza to cool for a few minutes before slicing and serving.

This Shrimp Scampi pizza is a delightful blend of garlicky shrimp and cheesy goodness. Enjoy this seafood-inspired pizza as a unique and tasty meal option!

Taco Pizza

Ingredients:

    Pizza dough (store-bought or homemade)
    Olive oil
    1 cup refried beans
    1 cup cooked and seasoned ground beef or shredded chicken
    1 cup shredded cheddar cheese
    1 cup shredded lettuce
    1 cup diced tomatoes
    1/2 cup sliced black olives
    1/4 cup sliced green onions
    Sour cream (for drizzling)
    Salsa (for serving)
    Taco seasoning (for seasoning meat)
    Salt and pepper to taste
    Fresh cilantro (optional, for garnish)

Instructions:

    Preheat your oven according to the pizza dough package instructions or your homemade dough recipe.
    Roll out the pizza dough on a floured surface to your desired thickness.
    Place the rolled-out dough on a pizza stone or a baking sheet.
    Brush the dough with olive oil to prevent sogginess.
    Spread an even layer of refried beans over the dough, leaving a small border around the edges.
    Cook and season the ground beef or shredded chicken with taco seasoning, salt, and pepper. Spread the seasoned meat over the refried beans.
    Sprinkle shredded cheddar cheese evenly over the meat layer.
    Bake the pizza in the preheated oven according to the dough instructions or until the crust is golden and the cheese is melted and bubbly.
    Once out of the oven, top the pizza with shredded lettuce, diced tomatoes, sliced black olives, and sliced green onions.
    Drizzle sour cream over the top and garnish with fresh cilantro if desired.
    Slice the taco pizza and serve with salsa on the side.

Enjoy your Taco Pizza, a fun and flavorful twist that combines the best of both tacos and pizza! Customize the toppings to suit your taste preferences.

Philly Cheesesteak Pizza

Ingredients:

    Pizza dough (store-bought or homemade)
    Olive oil
    1 cup sliced beefsteak or ribeye steak
    1 onion, thinly sliced
    1 bell pepper, thinly sliced
    1 cup shredded provolone cheese
    1 cup shredded mozzarella cheese
    Salt and black pepper to taste
    Garlic powder (optional)
    Pizza sauce (optional, for drizzling)
    Fresh parsley, chopped (for garnish)

Instructions:

    Preheat your oven according to the pizza dough package instructions or your homemade dough recipe.
    Roll out the pizza dough on a floured surface to your desired thickness.
    Place the rolled-out dough on a pizza stone or a baking sheet.
    In a skillet over medium heat, cook the sliced steak until browned. Add salt and black pepper to taste. Remove the steak from the skillet and set aside.
    In the same skillet, add a bit of olive oil and sauté the sliced onions and bell peppers until they are soft and slightly caramelized.
    Brush the pizza dough with olive oil to prevent sogginess.
    Spread a mixture of provolone and mozzarella cheese over the pizza dough.
    Distribute the cooked steak, sautéed onions, and bell peppers evenly over the cheese.
    Optionally, sprinkle a bit of garlic powder over the top for extra flavor.
    Bake the pizza in the preheated oven according to the dough instructions or until the crust is golden, and the cheese is melted and bubbly.
    Once out of the oven, drizzle a small amount of pizza sauce over the top if desired.
    Garnish with freshly chopped parsley.
    Allow the pizza to cool for a few minutes before slicing and serving.

Enjoy your Philly Cheesesteak pizza, a savory and satisfying combination of the iconic Philly Cheesesteak flavors on a pizza crust!

Breakfast Pizza with Eggs and Bacon

Ingredients:

    Pizza dough (store-bought or homemade)
    Olive oil
    1 cup shredded mozzarella cheese
    4 slices of bacon, cooked and crumbled
    4 large eggs
    Salt and black pepper to taste
    1/4 cup grated Parmesan cheese
    Fresh chives or green onions, chopped (for garnish)

Instructions:

    Preheat your oven according to the pizza dough package instructions or your homemade dough recipe.
    Roll out the pizza dough on a floured surface to your desired thickness.
    Place the rolled-out dough on a pizza stone or a baking sheet.
    Brush the dough with olive oil to prevent sogginess.
    Sprinkle the shredded mozzarella cheese evenly over the pizza dough.
    Cook the bacon until crispy, then crumble it and spread it over the cheese.
    Create wells in the cheese and bacon mixture to crack the eggs into.
    Carefully crack one egg into each well on the pizza.
    Season the eggs with salt and black pepper to taste.
    Bake the pizza in the preheated oven according to the dough instructions or until the crust is golden, the cheese is melted, and the eggs are cooked to your liking.
    Once out of the oven, sprinkle grated Parmesan cheese over the top.
    Garnish with fresh chives or green onions.
    Allow the pizza to cool for a few minutes before slicing and serving.

Enjoy your Breakfast Pizza with Eggs and Bacon, a delightful combination of classic breakfast ingredients on a pizza crust! Feel free to customize with additional toppings like tomatoes, spinach, or mushrooms, based on your preferences.

Artichoke and Olive Pizza

Ingredients:

  Pizza dough (store-bought or homemade)
  Olive oil
  1 cup pizza sauce (homemade or store-bought)
  1 cup shredded mozzarella cheese
  1 cup marinated artichoke hearts, drained and chopped
  1/2 cup Kalamata olives, sliced
  1/4 cup grated Parmesan cheese
  Red pepper flakes (optional, for added spice)
  Fresh basil or parsley, chopped (for garnish)

Instructions:

  Preheat your oven according to the pizza dough package instructions or your homemade dough recipe.
  Roll out the pizza dough on a floured surface to your desired thickness.
  Place the rolled-out dough on a pizza stone or a baking sheet.
  Brush the dough with olive oil to prevent sogginess.
  Spread an even layer of pizza sauce over the dough, leaving a small border around the edges.
  Sprinkle the shredded mozzarella cheese evenly over the sauce.
  Distribute the chopped artichoke hearts and sliced Kalamata olives over the cheese.
  Sprinkle grated Parmesan cheese over the top.
  Optional: Add red pepper flakes for a bit of heat.
  Bake the pizza in the preheated oven according to the dough instructions or until the crust is golden and the cheese is melted and bubbly.
  Once out of the oven, garnish with fresh basil or parsley.
  Allow the pizza to cool for a few minutes before slicing and serving.

This Artichoke and Olive Pizza offers a delicious combination of briny olives, tangy artichokes, and cheesy goodness. Customize it with your favorite herbs or additional toppings to suit your taste preferences. Enjoy!

Roasted Red Pepper and Goat Cheese Pizza

Ingredients:

>Pizza dough (store-bought or homemade)
>Olive oil
>1 cup roasted red peppers, sliced
>4 oz goat cheese, crumbled
>1 cup shredded mozzarella cheese
>1/4 cup grated Parmesan cheese
>2 cloves garlic, minced
>Fresh basil, chopped (for garnish)
>Salt and black pepper to taste
>Red pepper flakes (optional, for added spice)

Instructions:

>Preheat your oven according to the pizza dough package instructions or your homemade dough recipe.
>Roll out the pizza dough on a floured surface to your desired thickness.
>Place the rolled-out dough on a pizza stone or a baking sheet.
>Brush the dough with olive oil to prevent sogginess.
>Sprinkle the minced garlic evenly over the pizza dough.
>Spread an even layer of shredded mozzarella cheese over the dough.
>Distribute the sliced roasted red peppers over the cheese.
>Crumble the goat cheese evenly over the pizza.
>Sprinkle grated Parmesan cheese over the top.
>Season with salt and black pepper to taste. Add red pepper flakes if you like it spicy.
>Bake the pizza in the preheated oven according to the dough instructions or until the crust is golden and the cheese is melted and bubbly.
>Once out of the oven, garnish with fresh chopped basil.
>Allow the pizza to cool for a few minutes before slicing and serving.

This Roasted Red Pepper and Goat Cheese Pizza offers a unique blend of flavors with the sweetness of roasted red peppers and the tanginess of goat cheese. Customize it with additional toppings or herbs to suit your preferences. Enjoy!

Truffle Mushroom Pizza

Ingredients:

Pizza dough (store-bought or homemade)
Olive oil
1 cup shredded mozzarella cheese
1 cup sliced mushrooms (a mix of your favorite mushrooms such as cremini, shiitake, or oyster)
Truffle oil
2 cloves garlic, minced
Salt and black pepper to taste
Fresh thyme or parsley, chopped (for garnish)
Grated Parmesan cheese (optional, for finishing)

Instructions:

Preheat your oven according to the pizza dough package instructions or your homemade dough recipe.
Roll out the pizza dough on a floured surface to your desired thickness.
Place the rolled-out dough on a pizza stone or a baking sheet.
Brush the dough with olive oil to prevent sogginess.
Sprinkle the minced garlic evenly over the pizza dough.
Spread an even layer of shredded mozzarella cheese over the dough.
Distribute the sliced mushrooms evenly over the cheese.
Drizzle truffle oil over the pizza according to your taste preferences. Be mindful not to use too much, as truffle oil is potent.
Season with salt and black pepper to taste.
Optional: Sprinkle grated Parmesan cheese over the top for an extra layer of flavor.
Bake the pizza in the preheated oven according to the dough instructions or until the crust is golden and the cheese is melted and bubbly.
Once out of the oven, garnish with fresh chopped thyme or parsley.
Allow the pizza to cool for a few minutes before slicing and serving.

This Truffle Mushroom Pizza is a sophisticated and flavorful option, perfect for those who enjoy the rich taste of truffles and the earthiness of mushrooms. Customize it with your favorite mushroom varieties or additional toppings if desired. Enjoy!

Chicken Alfredo Pizza

Ingredients:

Pizza dough (store-bought or homemade)
Olive oil
1 cup cooked chicken breast, shredded or diced
1 cup Alfredo sauce (store-bought or homemade)
1 1/2 cups shredded mozzarella cheese
1/2 cup grated Parmesan cheese
2 cloves garlic, minced
Fresh parsley, chopped (for garnish)
Salt and black pepper to taste

Instructions:

Preheat your oven according to the pizza dough package instructions or your homemade dough recipe.
Roll out the pizza dough on a floured surface to your desired thickness.
Place the rolled-out dough on a pizza stone or a baking sheet.
Brush the dough with olive oil to prevent sogginess.
Spread an even layer of Alfredo sauce over the pizza dough, leaving a small border around the edges.
Sprinkle the minced garlic evenly over the Alfredo sauce.
Distribute the cooked chicken evenly over the Alfredo sauce.
Sprinkle shredded mozzarella and grated Parmesan cheese over the top.
Season with salt and black pepper to taste.
Bake the pizza in the preheated oven according to the dough instructions or until the crust is golden and the cheese is melted and bubbly.
Once out of the oven, garnish with fresh chopped parsley.
Allow the pizza to cool for a few minutes before slicing and serving.

This Chicken Alfredo Pizza is a rich and satisfying option, combining the creamy Alfredo sauce with tender chicken on a pizza crust. Customize it with additional toppings like spinach, sun-dried tomatoes, or mushrooms if you like. Enjoy!

Meat Lover's Pizza

Ingredients:

- Pizza dough (store-bought or homemade)
- Olive oil
- 1 cup pizza sauce (homemade or store-bought)
- 1 cup shredded mozzarella cheese
- 1/2 cup cooked and crumbled sausage
- 1/2 cup pepperoni slices
- 1/2 cup cooked and crumbled bacon
- 1/2 cup sliced ham or Canadian bacon
- 1/4 cup sliced black olives
- 1/4 cup sliced green bell peppers
- 1/4 cup sliced red onions
- 1/4 cup grated Parmesan cheese
- Dried oregano or Italian seasoning (optional, for sprinkling)

Instructions:

- Preheat your oven according to the pizza dough package instructions or your homemade dough recipe.
- Roll out the pizza dough on a floured surface to your desired thickness.
- Place the rolled-out dough on a pizza stone or a baking sheet.
- Brush the dough with olive oil to prevent sogginess.
- Spread an even layer of pizza sauce over the dough, leaving a small border around the edges.
- Sprinkle the shredded mozzarella cheese evenly over the sauce.
- Distribute the cooked and crumbled sausage, pepperoni slices, crumbled bacon, sliced ham or Canadian bacon, black olives, sliced green bell peppers, and sliced red onions evenly over the cheese.
- Sprinkle grated Parmesan cheese over the top.
- Optionally, sprinkle dried oregano or Italian seasoning for added flavor.
- Bake the pizza in the preheated oven according to the dough instructions or until the crust is golden and the cheese is melted and bubbly.
- Once out of the oven, let the pizza cool for a few minutes before slicing and serving.

This Meat Lover's Pizza is a carnivore's delight with a mix of flavorful meats. Feel free to customize with your favorite meats or additional toppings. Enjoy!

Caramelized Onion and Brie Pizza

Ingredients:

    Pizza dough (store-bought or homemade)
    Olive oil
    2 large onions, thinly sliced
    Salt and black pepper to taste
    1 tablespoon balsamic vinegar (optional)
    1 tablespoon brown sugar (optional)
    8 oz Brie cheese, rind removed and sliced
    Fresh thyme leaves, for garnish
    Arugula (optional, for topping)
    Balsamic glaze (optional, for drizzling)

Instructions:

Preheat your oven according to the pizza dough package instructions or your homemade dough recipe.
Roll out the pizza dough on a floured surface to your desired thickness.
Place the rolled-out dough on a pizza stone or a baking sheet.
In a skillet, heat olive oil over medium heat. Add the thinly sliced onions and cook, stirring occasionally, until they are soft and caramelized. Season with salt and black pepper.
Optional: Add balsamic vinegar and brown sugar to the caramelized onions for added depth of flavor. Cook for an additional 2-3 minutes until the mixture thickens slightly.
Brush the pizza dough with olive oil to prevent sogginess.
Spread the caramelized onions evenly over the pizza dough.
Arrange the sliced Brie cheese over the caramelized onions.
Bake the pizza in the preheated oven according to the dough instructions or until the crust is golden and the cheese is melted and bubbly.
Once out of the oven, garnish with fresh thyme leaves.
Optional: Top the pizza with a handful of arugula for a peppery kick.
Drizzle with balsamic glaze for an extra touch of sweetness and tanginess.
Allow the pizza to cool for a few minutes before slicing and serving.

This Caramelized Onion and Brie Pizza is an elegant and flavorful choice. Customize it with your preferred variations and enjoy the delightful combination of sweet caramelized onions and creamy brie cheese.

BLT Pizza

Ingredients:

    Pizza dough (store-bought or homemade)
    Olive oil
    1 cup shredded mozzarella cheese
    8 slices bacon, cooked and crumbled
    1 cup cherry tomatoes, halved
    1 cup shredded iceberg lettuce
    1/4 cup mayonnaise
    1 teaspoon Dijon mustard
    Salt and black pepper to taste
    Fresh basil or parsley, chopped (for garnish)

Instructions:

    Preheat your oven according to the pizza dough package instructions or your homemade dough recipe.
    Roll out the pizza dough on a floured surface to your desired thickness.
    Place the rolled-out dough on a pizza stone or a baking sheet.
    Brush the dough with olive oil to prevent sogginess.
    Sprinkle the shredded mozzarella cheese evenly over the pizza dough.
    Distribute the cooked and crumbled bacon over the cheese.
    Add the halved cherry tomatoes on top.
    Bake the pizza in the preheated oven according to the dough instructions or until the crust is golden and the cheese is melted and bubbly.
    While the pizza is baking, mix mayonnaise and Dijon mustard in a small bowl.
    Season with salt and black pepper to taste.
    Once out of the oven, spread the shredded iceberg lettuce over the hot pizza.
    Drizzle the mayonnaise and Dijon mixture over the lettuce.
    Garnish with fresh chopped basil or parsley.
    Allow the pizza to cool for a few minutes before slicing and serving.

This BLT Pizza captures the essence of the classic sandwich in a delightful and shareable format. Customize it with your preferred variations and enjoy the combination of crispy bacon, juicy tomatoes, and cool lettuce on a pizza crust.

Shrimp and Pesto Pizza

Ingredients:

    Pizza dough (store-bought or homemade)
    Olive oil
    1/2 cup pesto sauce (store-bought or homemade)
    1 cup cooked shrimp, peeled and deveined
    1 cup cherry tomatoes, halved
    1 cup shredded mozzarella cheese
    1/4 cup grated Parmesan cheese
    2 cloves garlic, minced
    Red pepper flakes (optional, for added spice)
    Fresh basil, chopped (for garnish)
    Lemon wedges (for serving)

Instructions:

    Preheat your oven according to the pizza dough package instructions or your homemade dough recipe.
    Roll out the pizza dough on a floured surface to your desired thickness.
    Place the rolled-out dough on a pizza stone or a baking sheet.
    Brush the dough with olive oil to prevent sogginess.
    Spread an even layer of pesto sauce over the pizza dough, leaving a small border around the edges.
    Sprinkle the minced garlic evenly over the pesto.
    Distribute the cooked shrimp and halved cherry tomatoes evenly over the pesto.
    Sprinkle shredded mozzarella and grated Parmesan cheese over the top.
    Optional: Add red pepper flakes for a bit of heat.
    Bake the pizza in the preheated oven according to the dough instructions or until the crust is golden and the cheese is melted and bubbly.
    Once out of the oven, garnish with fresh chopped basil.
    Allow the pizza to cool for a few minutes before slicing.
    Serve with lemon wedges for squeezing over the pizza before enjoying.

This Shrimp and Pesto Pizza offers a delightful combination of flavors. The pesto adds a burst of freshness, complementing the succulent shrimp and juicy cherry tomatoes.

Feel free to customize with additional toppings or herbs to suit your taste preferences.

Enjoy!

Margherita with Balsamic Glaze

Ingredients:

    Pizza dough (store-bought or homemade)
    Olive oil
    1 cup tomato sauce (homemade or store-bought)
    8 oz fresh mozzarella, sliced
    1 cup cherry tomatoes, halved
    Fresh basil leaves
    Salt and black pepper to taste
    Balsamic glaze

Instructions:

    Preheat your oven according to the pizza dough package instructions or your homemade dough recipe.
    Roll out the pizza dough on a floured surface to your desired thickness.
    Place the rolled-out dough on a pizza stone or a baking sheet.
    Brush the dough with olive oil to prevent sogginess.
    Spread an even layer of tomato sauce over the pizza dough, leaving a small border around the edges.
    Arrange slices of fresh mozzarella and halved cherry tomatoes over the tomato sauce.
    Season with salt and black pepper to taste.
    Bake the pizza in the preheated oven according to the dough instructions or until the crust is golden and the cheese is melted and bubbly.
    Once out of the oven, top the pizza with fresh basil leaves.
    Drizzle balsamic glaze over the pizza according to your taste preferences.
    Allow the pizza to cool for a few minutes before slicing and serving.

This Margherita Pizza with Balsamic Glaze is a delightful combination of the classic Margherita flavors with a sweet and tangy twist from the balsamic glaze. Customize it with additional toppings or herbs if desired. Enjoy!

Mediterranean Hummus Pizza

Ingredients:

Pizza dough (store-bought or homemade)
Olive oil
1 cup hummus (store-bought or homemade)
1 cup cherry tomatoes, halved
1/2 cup Kalamata olives, sliced
1/2 cup red onion, thinly sliced
1/2 cup feta cheese, crumbled
1/4 cup pine nuts (optional)
Fresh basil or parsley, chopped (for garnish)
Lemon wedges (for serving)

Instructions:

Preheat your oven according to the pizza dough package instructions or your homemade dough recipe.
Roll out the pizza dough on a floured surface to your desired thickness.
Place the rolled-out dough on a pizza stone or a baking sheet.
Brush the dough with olive oil to prevent sogginess.
Spread an even layer of hummus over the pizza dough, leaving a small border around the edges.
Arrange halved cherry tomatoes, sliced Kalamata olives, and thinly sliced red onions over the hummus.
Sprinkle crumbled feta cheese over the top.
Optional: Add pine nuts for an extra crunch.
Bake the pizza in the preheated oven according to the dough instructions or until the crust is golden and the toppings are heated through.
Once out of the oven, garnish with fresh chopped basil or parsley.
Serve with lemon wedges on the side for a squeeze of fresh lemon juice.
Allow the pizza to cool for a few minutes before slicing and serving.

This Mediterranean Hummus Pizza is a delightful combination of creamy hummus and vibrant Mediterranean flavors. Customize it with additional toppings such as artichoke hearts, sun-dried tomatoes, or roasted red peppers if desired. Enjoy!

Buffalo Cauliflower Pizza

Ingredients:

    Pizza dough (store-bought or homemade)
    Olive oil
    1 head of cauliflower, cut into florets
    1/2 cup buffalo sauce (homemade or store-bought)
    1 cup shredded mozzarella cheese
    1/4 cup crumbled blue cheese
    2 tablespoons ranch dressing (optional, for drizzling)
    Green onions, sliced (for garnish)
    Fresh cilantro or parsley, chopped (for garnish)
    Salt and black pepper to taste

Instructions:

    Preheat your oven according to the pizza dough package instructions or your homemade dough recipe.
    Toss the cauliflower florets in olive oil, salt, and black pepper. Roast in the oven at 425°F (220°C) for about 20-25 minutes or until they are tender and slightly browned.
    While the cauliflower is roasting, roll out the pizza dough on a floured surface to your desired thickness.
    Place the rolled-out dough on a pizza stone or a baking sheet.
    Brush the dough with olive oil to prevent sogginess.
    In a bowl, toss the roasted cauliflower in buffalo sauce until well coated.
    Spread an even layer of shredded mozzarella cheese over the pizza dough.
    Distribute the buffalo cauliflower evenly over the cheese.
    Sprinkle crumbled blue cheese on top.
    Bake the pizza in the preheated oven according to the dough instructions or until the crust is golden and the cheese is melted and bubbly.
    Once out of the oven, drizzle ranch dressing over the pizza if desired.
    Garnish with sliced green onions and chopped cilantro or parsley.
    Allow the pizza to cool for a few minutes before slicing and serving.

This Buffalo Cauliflower Pizza offers a spicy kick and a delicious combination of flavors. Customize it with additional toppings like red onion or jalapeños for extra heat if desired. Enjoy!

Greek Gyro Pizza

Ingredients:

- Pizza dough (store-bought or homemade)
- Olive oil
- Tzatziki sauce (store-bought or homemade)
- 1 cup cooked and thinly sliced gyro meat (beef, lamb, or a mix)
- 1 cup cherry tomatoes, halved
- 1/2 cup sliced red onion
- 1 cup crumbled feta cheese
- 1/4 cup sliced Kalamata olives
- 1 teaspoon dried oregano
- Salt and black pepper to taste
- Fresh parsley, chopped (for garnish)

Instructions:

1. Preheat your oven according to the pizza dough package instructions or your homemade dough recipe.
2. Roll out the pizza dough on a floured surface to your desired thickness.
3. Place the rolled-out dough on a pizza stone or a baking sheet.
4. Brush the dough with olive oil to prevent sogginess.
5. Spread an even layer of tzatziki sauce over the pizza dough, leaving a small border around the edges.
6. Distribute the cooked and thinly sliced gyro meat evenly over the tzatziki sauce.
7. Arrange halved cherry tomatoes, sliced red onion, and crumbled feta cheese over the gyro meat.
8. Sprinkle sliced Kalamata olives over the top.
9. Season with dried oregano, salt, and black pepper to taste.
10. Bake the pizza in the preheated oven according to the dough instructions or until the crust is golden and the toppings are heated through.
11. Once out of the oven, garnish with fresh chopped parsley.
12. Allow the pizza to cool for a few minutes before slicing and serving.

This Greek Gyro Pizza is a delightful fusion of Mediterranean flavors. Customize it with additional toppings like cucumber, red peppers, or artichoke hearts if desired. Enjoy!

BBQ Pulled Pork Pizza

Ingredients:

Pizza dough (store-bought or homemade)
Olive oil
1 cup barbecue sauce (store-bought or homemade)
1 cup cooked and shredded pulled pork
1 cup shredded mozzarella cheese
1/2 cup red onion, thinly sliced
1/4 cup fresh cilantro, chopped
1/4 cup pickled jalapeños (optional, for added heat)
Salt and black pepper to taste

Instructions:

Preheat your oven according to the pizza dough package instructions or your homemade dough recipe.
Roll out the pizza dough on a floured surface to your desired thickness.
Place the rolled-out dough on a pizza stone or a baking sheet.
Brush the dough with olive oil to prevent sogginess.
Spread an even layer of barbecue sauce over the pizza dough, leaving a small border around the edges.
Distribute the cooked and shredded pulled pork evenly over the barbecue sauce.
Sprinkle shredded mozzarella cheese over the pulled pork.
Scatter thinly sliced red onions over the cheese.
Optional: Add pickled jalapeños for a spicy kick.
Season with salt and black pepper to taste.
Bake the pizza in the preheated oven according to the dough instructions or until the crust is golden and the cheese is melted and bubbly.
Once out of the oven, sprinkle fresh chopped cilantro over the top.
Allow the pizza to cool for a few minutes before slicing and serving.

This BBQ Pulled Pork Pizza is a crowd-pleaser with a perfect balance of sweet and savory flavors. Customize it with additional toppings like pineapple, bell peppers, or even a drizzle of barbecue sauce on top if desired. Enjoy!

Thai Chicken Pizza

Ingredients:

    Pizza dough (store-bought or homemade)
    Peanut sauce (store-bought or homemade)
    1 cup cooked chicken breast, shredded or diced
    1 cup shredded mozzarella cheese
    1/2 cup shredded carrots
    1/2 cup red bell pepper, thinly sliced
    1/4 cup chopped green onions
    1/4 cup chopped cilantro
    1/4 cup chopped peanuts
    Lime wedges (for serving)

Instructions:

    Preheat your oven according to the pizza dough package instructions or your homemade dough recipe.
    Roll out the pizza dough on a floured surface to your desired thickness.
    Place the rolled-out dough on a pizza stone or a baking sheet.
    Spread an even layer of peanut sauce over the pizza dough, leaving a small border around the edges.
    Sprinkle shredded mozzarella cheese over the peanut sauce.
    Distribute the cooked and shredded chicken evenly over the cheese.
    Scatter shredded carrots and thinly sliced red bell pepper over the chicken.
    Bake the pizza in the preheated oven according to the dough instructions or until the crust is golden and the cheese is melted and bubbly.
    Once out of the oven, sprinkle chopped green onions, cilantro, and chopped peanuts over the top.
    Serve with lime wedges on the side for squeezing over the pizza before enjoying.

This Thai Chicken Pizza offers a unique blend of sweet, savory, and slightly spicy flavors. Customize it with additional toppings like bean sprouts, sliced jalapeños, or a drizzle of sriracha if desired. Enjoy the delicious fusion of Thai and Italian cuisines!

Caramelized Pear and Gorgonzola Pizza

Ingredients:

    Pizza dough (store-bought or homemade)
    Olive oil
    2 ripe pears, thinly sliced
    1 tablespoon unsalted butter
    2 tablespoons brown sugar
    1 cup crumbled Gorgonzola cheese
    1 cup shredded mozzarella cheese
    1/4 cup chopped walnuts
    Honey (for drizzling)
    Fresh thyme leaves (for garnish)
    Salt and black pepper to taste

Instructions:

    Preheat your oven according to the pizza dough package instructions or your homemade dough recipe.
    Roll out the pizza dough on a floured surface to your desired thickness.
    Place the rolled-out dough on a pizza stone or a baking sheet.
    In a skillet, melt butter over medium heat. Add the thinly sliced pears and brown sugar. Cook until the pears are caramelized, about 5-7 minutes. Set aside.
    Brush the pizza dough with olive oil to prevent sogginess.
    Spread an even layer of shredded mozzarella cheese over the pizza dough.
    Distribute the caramelized pears evenly over the cheese.
    Sprinkle crumbled Gorgonzola cheese and chopped walnuts over the top.
    Season with salt and black pepper to taste.
    Bake the pizza in the preheated oven according to the dough instructions or until the crust is golden and the cheese is melted and bubbly.
    Once out of the oven, drizzle honey over the pizza.
    Garnish with fresh thyme leaves.
    Allow the pizza to cool for a few minutes before slicing and serving.

This Caramelized Pear and Gorgonzola Pizza offers a perfect balance of sweetness from the pears, richness from the Gorgonzola, and a hint of nuttiness from the walnuts. Customize it with additional toppings or herbs to suit your taste preferences. Enjoy!

Smoked Salmon and Cream Cheese Pizza

Ingredients:

- Pizza dough (store-bought or homemade)
- Olive oil
- 1/2 cup cream cheese, softened
- 4 oz smoked salmon, thinly sliced
- 1/4 cup red onion, thinly sliced
- Capers, to taste
- Fresh dill, chopped (for garnish)
- Lemon wedges (for serving)

Instructions:

- Preheat your oven according to the pizza dough package instructions or your homemade dough recipe.
- Roll out the pizza dough on a floured surface to your desired thickness.
- Place the rolled-out dough on a pizza stone or a baking sheet.
- Brush the dough with olive oil to prevent sogginess.
- Spread an even layer of softened cream cheese over the pizza dough, leaving a small border around the edges.
- Arrange the smoked salmon slices over the cream cheese.
- Scatter thinly sliced red onions and capers over the smoked salmon.
- Bake the pizza in the preheated oven according to the dough instructions or until the crust is golden and the toppings are heated through.
- Once out of the oven, garnish with fresh chopped dill.
- Serve with lemon wedges on the side for squeezing over the pizza before enjoying.

This Smoked Salmon and Cream Cheese Pizza is a sophisticated and delicious option, perfect for brunch or as an elegant appetizer. Customize it with additional toppings like arugula or cherry tomatoes if desired. Enjoy the delightful combination of creamy cheese and smoky salmon!

Ratatouille Pizza

Ingredients:

- Pizza dough (store-bought or homemade)
- Olive oil
- 1 cup tomato sauce (homemade or store-bought)
- 1 small eggplant, thinly sliced
- 1 zucchini, thinly sliced
- 1 yellow bell pepper, thinly sliced
- 1 red onion, thinly sliced
- 2 tomatoes, thinly sliced
- 2 cloves garlic, minced
- 1 teaspoon dried thyme
- 1 teaspoon dried oregano
- Salt and black pepper to taste
- 1 cup shredded mozzarella cheese
- Fresh basil, chopped (for garnish)

Instructions:

- Preheat your oven according to the pizza dough package instructions or your homemade dough recipe.
- Roll out the pizza dough on a floured surface to your desired thickness.
- Place the rolled-out dough on a pizza stone or a baking sheet.
- Brush the dough with olive oil to prevent sogginess.
- Spread an even layer of tomato sauce over the pizza dough, leaving a small border around the edges.
- In a bowl, toss the thinly sliced eggplant, zucchini, yellow bell pepper, red onion, and tomatoes with minced garlic, dried thyme, dried oregano, salt, and black pepper.
- Arrange the seasoned vegetables evenly over the tomato sauce.
- Sprinkle shredded mozzarella cheese over the top.
- Bake the pizza in the preheated oven according to the dough instructions or until the crust is golden and the cheese is melted and bubbly.
- Once out of the oven, garnish with fresh chopped basil.
- Allow the pizza to cool for a few minutes before slicing and serving.

This Ratatouille Pizza captures the essence of the classic French dish on a pizza. The roasted vegetables combined with herbs and cheese create a flavorful and colorful dish. Enjoy the unique and delicious twist!

Chipotle BBQ Beef Pizza

Ingredients:

- Pizza dough (store-bought or homemade)
- Olive oil
- 1 cup barbecue sauce (store-bought or homemade)
- 1 tablespoon chipotle peppers in adobo sauce, finely chopped
- 1 cup cooked and shredded beef (such as brisket or roast beef)
- 1 cup shredded mozzarella cheese
- 1/2 cup red onion, thinly sliced
- 1/4 cup fresh cilantro, chopped
- 1/4 cup corn kernels (optional)
- 1/4 cup crumbled queso fresco or feta cheese
- Salt and black pepper to taste

Instructions:

1. Preheat your oven according to the pizza dough package instructions or your homemade dough recipe.
2. Roll out the pizza dough on a floured surface to your desired thickness.
3. Place the rolled-out dough on a pizza stone or a baking sheet.
4. Brush the dough with olive oil to prevent sogginess.
5. In a bowl, mix the barbecue sauce and finely chopped chipotle peppers.
6. Spread an even layer of the chipotle BBQ sauce over the pizza dough, leaving a small border around the edges.
7. Distribute the cooked and shredded beef evenly over the sauce.
8. Sprinkle shredded mozzarella cheese over the beef.
9. Scatter thinly sliced red onions, chopped cilantro, and corn kernels (if using) over the cheese.
10. Season with salt and black pepper to taste.
11. Crumble queso fresco or feta cheese over the top.
12. Bake the pizza in the preheated oven according to the dough instructions or until the crust is golden and the cheese is melted and bubbly.
13. Once out of the oven, let the pizza cool for a few minutes before slicing and serving.

This Chipotle BBQ Beef Pizza offers a bold and spicy flavor profile. Customize it with additional toppings like jalapeños or bell peppers for extra heat, or add sliced avocado or a drizzle of ranch dressing for a cool contrast. Enjoy the smoky goodness!

Bruschetta Pizza

Ingredients:

　　Pizza dough (store-bought or homemade)
　　Olive oil
　　3 large tomatoes, diced
　　2 cloves garlic, minced
　　1/4 cup fresh basil, chopped
　　1 cup shredded mozzarella cheese
　　Balsamic glaze (for drizzling, optional)
　　Salt and black pepper to taste
　　Grated Parmesan cheese (optional, for topping)
　　Fresh arugula (optional, for topping)

Instructions:

　　Preheat your oven according to the pizza dough package instructions or your homemade dough recipe.
　　Roll out the pizza dough on a floured surface to your desired thickness.
　　Place the rolled-out dough on a pizza stone or a baking sheet.
　　Brush the dough with olive oil to prevent sogginess.
　　In a bowl, combine diced tomatoes, minced garlic, and chopped fresh basil.
　　Season with salt and black pepper to taste.
　　Spread an even layer of the tomato mixture over the pizza dough, leaving a small border around the edges.
　　Sprinkle shredded mozzarella cheese over the tomato mixture.
　　Bake the pizza in the preheated oven according to the dough instructions or until the crust is golden and the cheese is melted and bubbly.
　　Once out of the oven, drizzle with balsamic glaze if desired.
　　Optional: Top with grated Parmesan cheese for extra flavor.
　　If you like, add a handful of fresh arugula on top for a peppery kick.
　　Allow the pizza to cool for a few minutes before slicing and serving.

This Bruschetta Pizza offers the classic flavors of bruschetta with the added goodness of melted cheese on a crispy crust. Customize it with additional toppings like olives or red onion if desired. Enjoy the fresh and vibrant taste!

Apple, Bacon, and Cheddar Pizza

Ingredients:

    Pizza dough (store-bought or homemade)
    Olive oil
    1 cup shredded sharp cheddar cheese
    1 large apple, thinly sliced (such as Granny Smith or Honeycrisp)
    6 slices bacon, cooked and crumbled
    1/4 cup red onion, thinly sliced
    2 tablespoons maple syrup
    1/4 cup chopped walnuts or pecans
    Fresh thyme leaves (for garnish)
    Salt and black pepper to taste

Instructions:

    Preheat your oven according to the pizza dough package instructions or your homemade dough recipe.
    Roll out the pizza dough on a floured surface to your desired thickness.
    Place the rolled-out dough on a pizza stone or a baking sheet.
    Brush the dough with olive oil to prevent sogginess.
    Sprinkle an even layer of shredded sharp cheddar cheese over the pizza dough.
    Arrange thinly sliced apples, crumbled bacon, and sliced red onions evenly over the cheese.
    Drizzle the maple syrup over the top.
    Sprinkle chopped walnuts or pecans on the pizza.
    Season with salt and black pepper to taste.
    Bake the pizza in the preheated oven according to the dough instructions or until the crust is golden and the cheese is melted and bubbly.
    Once out of the oven, garnish with fresh thyme leaves.
    Allow the pizza to cool for a few minutes before slicing and serving.

This Apple, Bacon, and Cheddar Pizza offers a delightful combination of sweet, salty, and savory flavors. Customize it with a drizzle of balsamic glaze or a sprinkle of blue cheese if desired. Enjoy the unique and delicious taste!

S'mores Dessert Pizza

Ingredients:

- Pizza dough (store-bought or homemade)
- Graham cracker crumbs
- Chocolate chips or chunks
- Mini marshmallows
- 2 tablespoons unsalted butter, melted
- 2 tablespoons honey or chocolate sauce (for drizzling, optional)

Instructions:

- Preheat your oven according to the pizza dough package instructions or your homemade dough recipe.
- Roll out the pizza dough on a floured surface to your desired thickness.
- Place the rolled-out dough on a pizza stone or a baking sheet.
- Brush the dough with melted unsalted butter.
- Sprinkle a generous amount of graham cracker crumbs over the buttered dough.
- Distribute chocolate chips or chunks evenly over the graham cracker crumbs.
- Scatter mini marshmallows over the chocolate.
- Bake the pizza in the preheated oven according to the dough instructions or until the crust is golden, and the marshmallows are toasted and gooey.
- Once out of the oven, drizzle honey or chocolate sauce over the top if desired.
- Allow the pizza to cool for a few minutes before slicing and serving.

This S'mores Dessert Pizza captures the essence of a classic s'more in a fun and shareable format. Customize it with additional toppings like chopped nuts or a sprinkle of sea salt if desired. Enjoy the gooey, chocolatey goodness!

Roasted Veggie and Pesto Pizza

Ingredients:

    Pizza dough (store-bought or homemade)
    Olive oil
    1/2 cup pesto sauce (store-bought or homemade)
    1 zucchini, thinly sliced
    1 bell pepper (any color), thinly sliced
    1 small eggplant, thinly sliced
    1 cup cherry tomatoes, halved
    1 red onion, thinly sliced
    1 cup shredded mozzarella cheese
    Salt and black pepper to taste
    Fresh basil, chopped (for garnish)

Instructions:

    Preheat your oven according to the pizza dough package instructions or your homemade dough recipe.
    Roll out the pizza dough on a floured surface to your desired thickness.
    Place the rolled-out dough on a pizza stone or a baking sheet.
    Brush the dough with olive oil to prevent sogginess.
    Spread an even layer of pesto sauce over the pizza dough, leaving a small border around the edges.
    In a bowl, toss the thinly sliced zucchini, bell pepper, eggplant, cherry tomatoes, and red onion with olive oil, salt, and black pepper.
    Arrange the seasoned vegetables evenly over the pesto.
    Sprinkle shredded mozzarella cheese over the vegetables.
    Bake the pizza in the preheated oven according to the dough instructions or until the crust is golden and the cheese is melted and bubbly.
    Once out of the oven, garnish with fresh chopped basil.
    Allow the pizza to cool for a few minutes before slicing and serving.

This Roasted Veggie and Pesto Pizza offers a burst of fresh and savory flavors.

Customize it with your favorite vegetables or add crumbled feta cheese for extra

richness. Enjoy the delicious and colorful combination!

Buffalo Cauliflower Ranch Pizza

Ingredients:

    Pizza dough (store-bought or homemade)
    Olive oil
    1 small head of cauliflower, cut into florets
    1/2 cup buffalo sauce (store-bought or homemade)
    1 cup shredded mozzarella cheese
    1/4 cup crumbled blue cheese
    2 tablespoons ranch dressing
    Green onions, sliced (for garnish)
    Fresh cilantro or parsley, chopped (for garnish)
    Salt and black pepper to taste

Instructions:

    Preheat your oven according to the pizza dough package instructions or your homemade dough recipe.
    Toss the cauliflower florets in olive oil, salt, and black pepper. Roast in the oven at 425°F (220°C) for about 20-25 minutes or until they are tender and slightly browned.
    While the cauliflower is roasting, roll out the pizza dough on a floured surface to your desired thickness.
    Place the rolled-out dough on a pizza stone or a baking sheet.
    Brush the dough with olive oil to prevent sogginess.
    In a bowl, toss the roasted cauliflower in buffalo sauce until well coated.
    Spread an even layer of shredded mozzarella cheese over the pizza dough.
    Distribute the buffalo cauliflower evenly over the cheese.
    Sprinkle crumbled blue cheese on top.
    Bake the pizza in the preheated oven according to the dough instructions or until the crust is golden and the cheese is melted and bubbly.
    Once out of the oven, drizzle ranch dressing over the pizza.
    Garnish with sliced green onions and chopped cilantro or parsley.
    Allow the pizza to cool for a few minutes before slicing and serving.

This Buffalo Cauliflower Ranch Pizza offers a perfect balance of spicy, tangy, and creamy flavors. Customize it with additional toppings like diced celery or jalapeños for added crunch and heat if desired. Enjoy the delicious twist on the classic buffalo flavor!

Chicken Tikka Masala Pizza

Ingredients:

    Pizza dough (store-bought or homemade)
    Chicken breast, cut into bite-sized pieces
    Yogurt
    Tikka masala spice blend or a mix of garam masala, cumin, coriander, and paprika
    Tomato sauce or puree
    Heavy cream or coconut milk
    Onion, thinly sliced
    Bell peppers, thinly sliced
    Mozzarella cheese, shredded
    Fresh cilantro, chopped (for garnish)

Instructions:

    Preheat your oven according to the pizza dough package instructions or your homemade dough recipe.
    Marinate the chicken pieces in yogurt and tikka masala spice blend for at least 30 minutes to an hour.
    In a pan, cook the marinated chicken until fully cooked and slightly charred.
    In a separate saucepan, prepare the tikka masala sauce by combining tomato sauce or puree with heavy cream or coconut milk. Season with additional tikka masala spices to taste.
    Roll out the pizza dough on a floured surface and transfer it to a pizza stone or baking sheet.
    Spread the tikka masala sauce over the pizza dough.
    Add the cooked chicken pieces, sliced onions, and bell peppers on top of the sauce.
    Sprinkle shredded mozzarella cheese over the pizza.
    Bake in the preheated oven according to the pizza dough instructions or until the crust is golden and the cheese is melted and bubbly.
    Remove the pizza from the oven, sprinkle chopped cilantro on top for freshness, and let it cool for a few minutes before slicing.

Enjoy your unique and delicious Chicken Tikka Masala Pizza!

Pear and Prosciutto Pizza

Ingredients:

    Pizza dough (store-bought or homemade)
    Olive oil
    Goat cheese or gorgonzola cheese, crumbled
    Mozzarella cheese, shredded
    Ripe pears, thinly sliced
    Prosciutto, thinly sliced
    Balsamic glaze (optional, for drizzling)
    Arugula (optional, for garnish)

Instructions:

1. Preheat your oven according to the pizza dough package instructions or your homemade dough recipe.
2. Roll out the pizza dough on a floured surface and transfer it to a pizza stone or baking sheet.
3. Brush the rolled-out dough with olive oil to prevent it from becoming soggy during baking.
4. Sprinkle a layer of mozzarella cheese over the pizza dough, leaving a border around the edges for the crust.
5. Distribute the crumbled goat cheese or gorgonzola evenly over the mozzarella.
6. Arrange the thinly sliced pears and prosciutto on top of the cheese.
7. Bake in the preheated oven according to the pizza dough instructions or until the crust is golden and the cheese is melted and bubbly.
8. Optional: Once the pizza is out of the oven, drizzle it with balsamic glaze for an extra layer of flavor.
9. If desired, garnish the pizza with fresh arugula just before serving. The peppery arugula adds a nice contrast to the sweetness of the pears and the saltiness of the prosciutto.
10. Allow the pizza to cool for a few minutes before slicing.

This Pear and Prosciutto Pizza makes for a sophisticated and delicious meal, perfect for a casual dinner or entertaining guests. Enjoy!

Spinach and Artichoke Dip Pizza

Ingredients:

    Pizza dough (store-bought or homemade)
    Olive oil
    Cream cheese, softened
    Sour cream
    Garlic, minced
    Frozen chopped spinach, thawed and squeezed dry
    Artichoke hearts, chopped
    Mozzarella cheese, shredded
    Parmesan cheese, grated
    Salt and pepper to taste
    Red pepper flakes (optional, for added heat)
    Fresh parsley, chopped (for garnish)

Instructions:

    Preheat your oven according to the pizza dough package instructions or your homemade dough recipe.
    Roll out the pizza dough on a floured surface and transfer it to a pizza stone or baking sheet.
    In a bowl, mix together cream cheese, sour cream, minced garlic, salt, and pepper until well combined.
    Spread the cream cheese mixture evenly over the rolled-out pizza dough, leaving a border for the crust.
    Distribute the thawed and squeezed dry chopped spinach and chopped artichoke hearts over the cream cheese layer.
    Sprinkle a generous amount of shredded mozzarella and grated Parmesan cheese over the top.
    If desired, sprinkle red pepper flakes for a bit of heat.
    Bake in the preheated oven according to the pizza dough instructions or until the crust is golden and the cheese is melted and bubbly.
    Once out of the oven, garnish the pizza with freshly chopped parsley for a burst of freshness.
    Allow the pizza to cool for a few minutes before slicing.

This Spinach and Artichoke Dip Pizza is a great option for parties or as a comforting and flavorful meal. Enjoy the creamy, cheesy goodness!

Caramelized Apple and Brie Dessert Pizza

Ingredients:

    Pizza dough (store-bought or homemade)
    Unsalted butter
    Apples (such as Granny Smith), peeled, cored, and thinly sliced
    Brown sugar
    Cinnamon
    Brie cheese, thinly sliced
    Honey (for drizzling)
    Chopped walnuts or pecans (optional, for added crunch)

Instructions:

    Preheat your oven according to the pizza dough package instructions or your homemade dough recipe.
    In a skillet over medium heat, melt a tablespoon of unsalted butter.
    Add the thinly sliced apples to the skillet and cook until they begin to soften.
    Sprinkle brown sugar and cinnamon over the apples, stirring to coat evenly.
    Continue cooking until the apples are caramelized and tender. Remove from heat.
    Roll out the pizza dough on a floured surface and transfer it to a pizza stone or baking sheet.
    Arrange the caramelized apples evenly over the pizza dough.
    Place thin slices of brie cheese on top of the apples.
    Optional: Sprinkle chopped walnuts or pecans over the pizza for added crunch.
    Bake in the preheated oven according to the pizza dough instructions or until the crust is golden and the cheese is melted and bubbly.
    Once out of the oven, drizzle honey over the top for an extra touch of sweetness.
    Allow the dessert pizza to cool for a few minutes before slicing.

This Caramelized Apple and Brie Dessert Pizza makes for a sophisticated and delicious end to a meal. The combination of warm caramelized apples, creamy brie, and honey creates a delightful flavor profile. Enjoy!

Caprese with Pesto Drizzle

Ingredients:

    Fresh tomatoes, sliced
    Fresh mozzarella cheese, sliced
    Fresh basil leaves
    Extra-virgin olive oil
    Balsamic glaze
    Salt and pepper to taste
    Pesto sauce (store-bought or homemade)

Instructions:

    Arrange the slices of fresh tomatoes and mozzarella cheese alternately on a serving platter.
    Tuck fresh basil leaves between the tomato and mozzarella slices.
    In a small bowl, whisk together extra-virgin olive oil, balsamic glaze, salt, and pepper. Adjust the quantities to suit your taste.
    Drizzle the olive oil and balsamic mixture over the arranged Caprese salad.
    Optionally, warm up the pesto sauce slightly to make it more drizzle-friendly.
    Drizzle the pesto sauce over the Caprese salad.
    If desired, garnish with additional fresh basil leaves.
    Serve immediately and enjoy the vibrant flavors of this Caprese with Pesto Drizzle.

This dish is not only visually appealing but also a delicious way to enjoy the classic Caprese combination with an added burst of pesto flavor. It makes a great appetizer or side dish, especially during the warmer months when fresh, ripe tomatoes and basil are in abundance.

Mediterranean Chicken Flatbread

Ingredients:

- Flatbread or naan (store-bought or homemade)
- Cooked chicken breast, shredded or sliced
- Hummus
- Cherry tomatoes, halved
- Cucumber, thinly sliced
- Kalamata olives, pitted and sliced
- Red onion, thinly sliced
- Feta cheese, crumbled
- Fresh parsley, chopped
- Extra-virgin olive oil
- Lemon wedges (optional, for serving)
- Salt and pepper to taste

Instructions:

1. Preheat your oven according to the flatbread or naan package instructions or your homemade flatbread recipe.
2. If the flatbread or naan is not pre-cooked, bake it in the preheated oven until it's slightly crispy.
3. Spread a generous layer of hummus over the flatbread.
4. Arrange the cooked chicken evenly over the hummus.
5. Scatter halved cherry tomatoes, thinly sliced cucumber, sliced Kalamata olives, and thinly sliced red onion over the flatbread.
6. Sprinkle crumbled feta cheese over the top.
7. Drizzle extra-virgin olive oil over the entire flatbread.
8. Season with salt and pepper to taste.
9. Bake in the preheated oven for a few minutes, just until the flatbread is heated through and the toppings are warmed.
10. Remove from the oven and sprinkle freshly chopped parsley over the top.
11. Optionally, squeeze lemon wedges over the flatbread before serving for a burst of citrus freshness.
12. Slice and serve your Mediterranean Chicken Flatbread immediately.

This dish offers a delightful combination of textures and flavors, with the creamy hummus, tender chicken, crisp vegetables, and the salty kick from feta and olives. It's a perfect option for a quick and satisfying lunch or dinner.

Roasted Garlic and Potato Pizza

Ingredients:

    Pizza dough (store-bought or homemade)
    Olive oil
    Roasted garlic cloves (see note below)
    Potatoes, thinly sliced (use a mandolin for even slices)
    Mozzarella cheese, shredded
    Parmesan cheese, grated
    Fresh rosemary, chopped
    Salt and pepper to taste
    Red pepper flakes (optional, for added heat)
    Cornmeal or flour (for dusting)

For Roasted Garlic:

- Whole garlic bulb
- Olive oil

Instructions:

Preheat your oven according to the pizza dough package instructions or your homemade dough recipe.
If you haven't already roasted garlic, preheat your oven to 400°F (200°C).
To roast garlic:
- Cut the top off a garlic bulb to expose the cloves.
- Place the bulb on a piece of foil, drizzle with olive oil, and wrap it tightly.
- Roast in the preheated oven for about 30-40 minutes or until the garlic is soft and golden. Allow it to cool before squeezing out the roasted cloves.

Roll out the pizza dough on a floured surface and transfer it to a pizza stone or baking sheet dusted with cornmeal or flour.
Brush the rolled-out dough with olive oil.
Spread the roasted garlic cloves evenly over the pizza dough.
Arrange the thinly sliced potatoes on top of the garlic.
Sprinkle shredded mozzarella and grated Parmesan cheese over the potatoes.
Season with chopped fresh rosemary, salt, and pepper. Add red pepper flakes if you like it spicy.

Bake in the preheated oven according to the pizza dough instructions or until the crust is golden and the cheese is melted and bubbly.
Allow the pizza to cool for a few minutes before slicing.

This Roasted Garlic and Potato Pizza offers a unique and comforting flavor profile. The roasted garlic adds a rich, mellow taste, and the thinly sliced potatoes provide a satisfying texture. Enjoy this delicious pizza as a main course or share it as an appetizer.

Fig, Prosciutto, and Gorgonzola Flatbread

Ingredients:

- Flatbread or naan (store-bought or homemade)
- Olive oil
- Fig preserves or fresh figs, sliced
- Prosciutto, thinly sliced
- Gorgonzola cheese, crumbled
- Arugula (optional, for garnish)
- Balsamic glaze (optional, for drizzling)
- Black pepper (optional, for seasoning)

Instructions:

1. Preheat your oven according to the flatbread or naan package instructions or your homemade flatbread recipe.
2. If the flatbread or naan is not pre-cooked, bake it in the preheated oven until it's slightly crispy.
3. Brush the flatbread with olive oil.
4. Spread a layer of fig preserves over the flatbread or arrange fresh fig slices evenly.
5. Lay slices of prosciutto over the fig layer.
6. Sprinkle crumbled Gorgonzola cheese over the prosciutto.
7. Optional: Season with black pepper for added flavor.
8. Bake in the preheated oven for a few minutes, just until the flatbread is heated through and the toppings are warmed.
9. If desired, garnish with fresh arugula for a peppery contrast.
10. Optionally, drizzle balsamic glaze over the flatbread before serving for an extra touch of sweetness and acidity.
11. Slice and serve your Fig, Prosciutto, and Gorgonzola Flatbread immediately.

This flatbread offers a harmonious blend of flavors, with the sweetness of figs, the savory richness of prosciutto, and the creaminess of Gorgonzola. It's a perfect appetizer for a gathering or a sophisticated yet easy-to-make meal. Enjoy!

Zucchini and Goat Cheese Pizza

Ingredients:

- Pizza dough (store-bought or homemade)
- Olive oil
- Zucchini, thinly sliced
- Goat cheese, crumbled
- Red onion, thinly sliced (optional)
- Fresh thyme or rosemary, chopped
- Salt and pepper to taste
- Crushed red pepper flakes (optional, for added heat)
- Balsamic glaze (optional, for drizzling)
- Parmesan cheese, grated (optional)

Instructions:

- Preheat your oven according to the pizza dough package instructions or your homemade dough recipe.
- Roll out the pizza dough on a floured surface and transfer it to a pizza stone or baking sheet.
- Brush the rolled-out dough with olive oil.
- Arrange the thinly sliced zucchini evenly over the pizza dough.
- Crumble goat cheese over the zucchini slices.
- If using, add thinly sliced red onions over the pizza.
- Sprinkle chopped fresh thyme or rosemary over the toppings.
- Season with salt and pepper to taste. Add crushed red pepper flakes if you like it spicy.
- Bake in the preheated oven according to the pizza dough instructions or until the crust is golden and the cheese is melted and bubbly.
- Optional: Drizzle balsamic glaze over the pizza for an extra layer of flavor.
- If desired, sprinkle grated Parmesan cheese over the top before serving.
- Allow the pizza to cool for a few minutes before slicing.

This Zucchini and Goat Cheese Pizza is a light and refreshing option, perfect for a quick and tasty dinner. The combination of the creamy goat cheese with the fresh zucchini and herbs creates a delightful medley of flavors. Enjoy!

Pumpkin and Sage Pizza

Ingredients:

- Pizza dough (store-bought or homemade)
- Olive oil
- Pumpkin puree (canned or homemade)
- Fresh sage leaves
- Mozzarella cheese, shredded
- Parmesan cheese, grated
- Salt and pepper to taste
- Nutmeg (optional, for a warm flavor)
- Red pepper flakes (optional, for added heat)
- Balsamic glaze (optional, for drizzling)

Instructions:

1. Preheat your oven according to the pizza dough package instructions or your homemade dough recipe.
2. Roll out the pizza dough on a floured surface and transfer it to a pizza stone or baking sheet.
3. Brush the rolled-out dough with olive oil.
4. Spread a layer of pumpkin puree evenly over the pizza dough.
5. Sprinkle shredded mozzarella and grated Parmesan cheese over the pumpkin layer.
6. Place fresh sage leaves on top of the cheese, distributing them evenly.
7. Season with salt, pepper, and optionally a pinch of nutmeg for a warm, aromatic flavor.
8. If you like a bit of heat, add red pepper flakes over the toppings.
9. Bake in the preheated oven according to the pizza dough instructions or until the crust is golden, and the cheese is melted and bubbly.
10. Optional: Drizzle balsamic glaze over the pizza for a touch of sweetness and acidity.
11. Allow the pizza to cool for a few minutes before slicing.

This Pumpkin and Sage Pizza is a comforting and flavorful option, perfect for fall or any time you're in the mood for a unique and delicious pizza experience. Enjoy the seasonal flavors!

www.ingramcontent.com/pod-product-compliance
Lightning Source LLC
LaVergne TN
LVHW061947070526
838199LV00060B/4010